FACT CAT

EGGS AND DAIRY

Izzi Howell

WAYLAND

www.waylandbooks.co.uk

FACT CAT

Get your paws on this fantastic new mega-series from Wayland!

Join our Fact Cat on a journey of fun learning about every subject under the sun!

First published in Great Britain in 2017 by Wayland
Copyright © Hodder and Stoughton Limited, 2017

ISBN: 978 1 5263 0380 6

10 9 8 7 6 5 4 3 2 1

MIX
Paper from
responsible sources
FSC® C104740

Wayland
An imprint of Hachette Children's Group
Part of Hodder & Stoughton
Carmelite House
50 Victoria Embankment
London EC4Y 0DZ

An Hachette UK Company
www.hachette.co.uk
www.hachettechildrens.co.uk

A catalogue for this title is available from
the British Library
Printed and bound in China

Produced for Wayland by
White-Thomson Publishing Ltd
www.wtpub.co.uk

Editor: Izzi Howell
Design: Clare Nicholas
Fact Cat illustrations: Shutterstock/Julien Troneur
Other illustrations: Stefan Chabluk
Consultant: Karina Philip

Picture and illustration credits:
iStock: Zvozdochka 11l, rvimages 12, nimu1956 13t, Kemter 13b, kali9 16, FatCamera 17, rez-art 18, DPimborough 20r; Shutterstock: Nitr cover, Jiri Hera title page and 14, Oleksandra Naumenko 4, MaraZe 5, mosista 6, Thawornnurak 7t, Ronnachai Palas 7b, Floortje 8t, Michael A. Bennett 8b, Gamzova Olga 9, Matee Nuserm 10, Ratthaphong Ekariyasap 11r, Joe Gough 15, Wanwisspaul 19, Jakub Cejpek 20l, mehmetcan 21t, JIANG HONGYAN 21b. Should there be any inadvertent omission, please apply to the publisher for rectification.

The author, Izzi Howell, is a writer and editor specialising in children's educational publishing.

The consultant, Karina Philip, is a teacher and a primary literacy consultant with an MA in creative writing.

FACT CAT FACT

There is a question for you to answer on most spreads in this book. You can check your answers on page 24.

CONTENTS

WHAT ARE EGGS AND DAIRY?

Eggs and dairy products are types of food. Eggs come from birds, such as chickens. Dairy products include milk, and foods made from milk, such as cheese.

Cheese, milk, cream, butter, cottage cheese and yoghurt are all dairy products.

cheese

milk

cream

yoghurt

cottage cheese

butter

Most people eat eggs and dairy products every day. You can eat eggs and dairy products, along with other foods, as part of a **balanced diet**.

FACT CAT FACT

Some people can't or don't eat dairy products. Dairy products can make some people feel ill. **Vegan** people choose not to eat eggs and dairy products because they don't want to eat anything that comes from an animal.

DIFFERENT EGGS

Most of the eggs that we eat come from chickens. Only hens (**female** chickens) lay eggs. Some supermarkets sell duck eggs and **quail** eggs.

All eggs have the same shape. They can be different colours and sizes. Which bird lays the largest eggs on Earth?

quail egg

duck egg

chicken egg

chicken egg

FACT CAT FACT

Chickens with brown feathers usually lay brown eggs. Most white eggs come from white chickens.

Inside the hard shell of an egg, there is egg white and egg **yolk**. Raw egg white is **transparent**. It turns white when it is cooked.

cooked egg

raw egg

Egg yolks are bright yellow when they are raw and when they are cooked.

DAIRY PRODUCTS

Most of the dairy products that we eat, such as butter, cheese and yoghurt, are made from cow's milk. Milk comes from female **mammals**, such as cows and goats.

Milk from goats is used to make goat's cheese.

Dairy products usually have a **mild flavour**. They taste creamy because they contain fat. Milk that has some of the fat removed is called semi-skimmed milk. Skimmed milk contains almost no fat.

Butter is almost entirely made of fat. This gives it a rich flavour.

Mozzarella cheese is traditionally made from buffalo milk. In Scandinavia, some cheeses are made from moose and reindeer milk!

ON THE FARM

Farmers **raise** chickens and dairy animals on farms. They feed the animals and keep them safe and warm.

The best farms allow their animals to move around freely. We use the word **free-range** to describe eggs and milk that come from these animals.

Most chickens lay an egg every day. Farmers milk cows twice a day. They put some of the milk into bottles to be sold in the supermarket. The rest is made into dairy products.

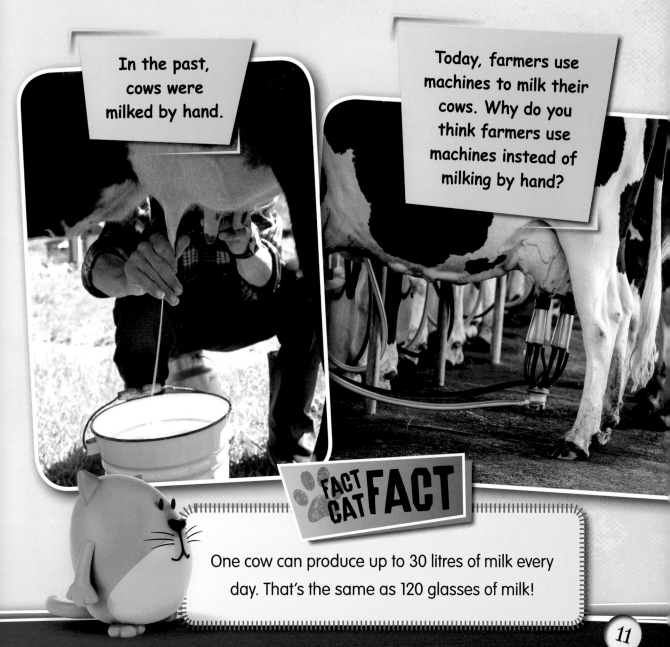

In the past, cows were milked by hand.

Today, farmers use machines to milk their cows. Why do you think farmers use machines instead of milking by hand?

FACT CAT FACT

One cow can produce up to 30 litres of milk every day. That's the same as 120 glasses of milk!

MAKING DAIRY PRODUCTS

There are several ways to change milk into dairy products. Butter is made by shaking milk or cream. Eventually, the fat from the milk comes together to form butter.

This Indian woman is preparing butter. The stick in the lid of the pot helps to move the milk around.

To make cheese, you heat milk and add a special ingredient called **rennet**. This makes the milk split into a **solid** part and a **liquid** part. The solid parts are squished together into cheese.

This cheese has just been made. The leftover liquid from the milk is still in the pan.

Some types of cheese are left for a long time before they are eaten. This gives them a better flavour.

COOKING

Eggs can be cooked in different ways. You can crack open eggs and fry them in a saucepan. **Poached** eggs are made by cracking an egg into a saucepan of **boiling** water.

A soft-boiled egg has a runny yolk. It was cooked inside its shell. What is the yolk of a hard-boiled egg like?

Dairy products don't need to be cooked before they are eaten. We eat slices of cheese in sandwiches. Yoghurt and fruit makes a good snack. However, there are cooked dishes that contain dairy products.

The sauce on this cauliflower cheese is made by cooking milk and butter with flour.

FACT CAT **FACT**

If you heat butter, it **melts** into a liquid like oil.
We often fry meat and vegetables in melted butter.

PROTEIN AND CALCIUM

Eggs and dairy products contain **protein**. Eating protein helps you develop muscles and keeps you strong.

Protein helps you to grow taller. Find out another food that contains protein.

Eating dairy products helps your body to get enough **calcium**. Your body needs calcium to keep your bones and teeth healthy.

You need strong bones to be able to run, jump and play.

FACT CAT FACT

You can also get calcium from nuts, beans and even seaweed!

A BALANCED DIET

You need to eat food from different food groups to have a balanced diet. Eggs and dairy products are an example of a food group.

A plate of spaghetti and meatballs contains food from different food groups. There is meat in the meatballs, spaghetti made from flour and vegetables in the sauce. Which part of the meal is a dairy product?

This diagram shows you how much of each type of food you should eat. The large parts of the circle show foods you should eat at most meals. The small parts of the circle show foods you should eat less often.

Fruit and vegetables

Grains and cereals

Meat, fish and eggs

Oil and butter

Dairy products

Eggs and dairy products are in these parts of the circle. You should eat them every day.

AROUND THE WORLD

People eat eggs and dairy products in countries around the world. In some places, they eat milk and eggs from animals that only live in their **local** area.

This woman from **Tibet** is milking a yak.

In Tibet, people drink tea mixed with butter made from yak's milk.

Eggs and dairy products are prepared in different ways around the world. In India, they add boiled eggs to spicy curries. In Mexico, they eat eggs with **tortillas**, beans and tomatoes for breakfast.

FACT CAT FACT

Ayran is a cold drink from Turkey. It is made by mixing yoghurt with water and salt.

This is a century egg. Century eggs are made by covering eggs in salt and clay. They are left for several weeks or even months. Which country do they come from?

QUIZ

Try to answer the questions below. Look back through the book to help you. Check your answers on page 24.

1 Which of these foods is a dairy product?

a) cheese

b) potatoes

c) eggs

2 Duck eggs are blue. True or not true?

a) true

b) not true

3 Egg whites turn yellow when they are cooked. True or not true?

a) true

b) not true

4 Which cheese is made from buffalo milk?

a) blue cheese

b) cottage cheese

c) mozzarella

5 How often do chickens lay eggs?

a) three times a day

b) once a day

c) once a week

6 Calcium is good for your bones. True or not true?

a) true

b) not true

GLOSSARY

balanced diet a diet that has a healthy mixture of different foods

boiling boiling water is very hot and bubbling

calcium something that is in food that helps your bones and teeth to be strong

female describes a woman

flavour the taste of a food or drink

free-range describes an animal that can move around outside and isn't kept in a cage

liquid something that is not a solid or a gas, such as milk

local describes something that comes from the area near you

mammal a type of animal with fur that gives birth to live young

melt to turn from a solid to a liquid

mild describes a flavour that isn't strong

mould a green or grey substance that grows on old food

muscles the parts of your body that are attached to bones and help you to move around

poached a poached egg has been cooked without its shell in water

protein something that is in food that helps the body to grow and be strong

quail a small brown bird

raise to look after an animal and help it to grow bigger

raw not cooked

rennet a liquid used in the making of cheese

solid something that is not a liquid or a gas, such as a table

Tibet an area in the high mountains of Asia

tortilla a corn pancake originally from Mexico

transparent see-through

vegan someone who doesn't eat any animal products, such as meat, fish, eggs or dairy products

yak a type of cattle with long hair that lives in the mountains of Asia

yolk the yellow part inside an egg

INDEX

ANSWERS

Pages 4–20

Page 5: Some foods include butter on toast and yoghurt with cereal.

Page 6: Ostrich

Page 11: Because it is much faster and easier to milk cows with a machine.

Page 14: Solid and not runny

Page 16: Some foods include meat, fish and nuts.

Page 18: Cheese

Page 21: China

Quiz answers

1   a - cheese

2   true

3   not true – egg whites are white when they have been cooked.

4   c - mozzarella

5   b – once a day

6   true

OTHER TITLES IN THE FACT CAT SERIES...

WAYLAND
www.waylandbooks.co.uk